writing guides

ACTIVITIES

Realistic STORIES

STORIES THAT RAISE ISSUES

ALISON KELLY

PHOTOCOPIABLE PHOTOC

FICTION FOR AGES 9-11

CONTENTS

INTRODUCTION

The Scholastic *Writing Guides* series provides teachers with ideas and projects that promote a range of writing, bringing insights from educational research into the classroom. Each guide explores a different type of writing and provides example material, background information, photocopiable activities and teaching suggestions. Their aim is to enable teachers to guide the writing process, share planning ideas and develop themes as a context for writing activities.

The materials:
- motivate children with interesting activities
- break complex types of writing into manageable teaching units
- focus on and develop the typical features of particular types of writing
- provide original approaches to teaching.

Each book is divided into sections, beginning with examples of the type of writing being taught. These are followed by ideas for developing writing and projects that will extend over a series of sessions.

SECTION ONE: USING GOOD EXAMPLES

Section One looks at good examples of the genre, with the emphasis on using texts to stimulate and develop writing. Two example texts are shared, and questions that focus the discussion on their significant features are suggested. This is followed by activities that explore what the texts can teach us about writing, enabling teachers to compare the two texts and to go on to model the type of writing presented in the guide.

SECTION TWO: DEVELOPING WRITING

Section Two moves from reading to writing. This section provides activities that prompt and support children in planning and writing. A range of approaches includes planning templates and strategies to stimulate ideas. The activities refine children's ideas about the type of writing being developed and give them focused writing practice in the context of scaffolded tasks. Teacher's notes support each activity by explaining the objective and giving guidance on delivery.

SECTION THREE: WRITING

Section Three moves on to writing projects. Building upon the earlier work in Section Two, these projects aim to develop the quality of writing and provide a selection of ideas for class or group work on a particular theme or idea. The teacher may choose to use some or all of the ideas presented in each project as a way of weaving the strategies developed in Section Two into a more complex and extended writing task.

SECTION FOUR: REVIEW

Section Four supports the assessment process. Children are encouraged to reflect on the type of writing they are tackling and to evaluate how effectively their work has met the criteria for the genre identified in Section One.

The Suitcase Kid

When my parents split up they didn't know what to do with me. My mum wanted me to go and live with her. My dad wanted me to go and live with him. I didn't want to go and live at my mum's new place or my dad's new place. I wanted to stay living in our *old* place, Mulberry Cottage, the three of us together. Four, counting my pet Sylvanian family spotted rabbit Radish.

There were all these arguments about who would get custody of me. I thought they were talking about custard at first. I hate custard because you can never tell when there's going to be a lump and it sticks in your throat and makes you shudder.

My mum got mad and my dad got mad and I got mad too. I felt *I* was being split up. Half of me wanted to side with Mum. Half of me wanted to side with Dad. It was much easier for Radish. She just sided with me. She lives in my pocket so there's never been any hassle over who gets custody of her.

We had to go for family counselling…

The counsellor saw me fiddling about in my pocket and she got a glimpse of Radish. I like to hold her tight when I'm feeling funny.

"Oh, what a dear little toy. Do let me have a look," she said, in that silly voice grown-ups always use when they're trying to get you to like them…

You'd have thought I was two years old, not ten. I just shrugged and shook my head.

"That's Radish," said Mum. "Andrea's had her for years and years. She's a very important member of our family."

"Actually, I bought Radish for Andrea. As a silly Saturday present. I like to give her a little treat every now and then," said Dad.

"You did not give Andrea Radish! *I* bought her one Christmas to go in Andrea's stocking," said Mum.

"Look, I can vividly remember buying that rabbit in the corner shop—"

"They don't even sell Sylvanian families at the corner shop. I bought it from the toy shop in town and—"

I snatched Radish back and put my hand gently over her ears. She can't stand to hear them arguing.

from *The Suitcase Kid* by Jacqueline Wilson.

The Battle of Bubble and Squeak

In his school trousers and his pyjama top, Sid flew downstairs. His mother met him at the bottom of the stairs. Tears were streaming down her cheeks; she also looked unspeakably angry. "Come and see what your – your THINGS have done!"

She dragged him into the living room. The room was still in semi-darkness because the curtains had not yet been drawn back. But the gloom was shot by strong beams of light coming through two large ragged holes in the curtains. The holes were just behind the cage, and by the light through them Sid could see that the inside of the gerbil cage was littered with scraps and crumbs of scarlet. One gerbil, sitting up watchfully, seemed to be wiping its mouth free of a scarlet thread.

"They've eaten my best curtains," said Mrs Sparrow.

Peggy had followed Sid, and now Amy and Bill Sparrow were crowding to see, Amy holding tight to Bill.

Amy peeped and peered. "I didn't know gerbils ate curtains."

"They don't *eat* them," said Peggy. 'They just gnaw at them.'

"They've ruined them," said Mrs Sparrow.

"Can't you mend them?" asked Bill Sparrow.

"Can't *I* mend them!"

"I'll mend them," said Sid. "I'll draw the edges of the holes together. I saw you mending that tear in my duffle coat, when it had caught on the barbed wire. I'll buy red cotton exactly to match, and I'll mend it. Peggy'll help me, won't you, Peg?"

"Yes," said Peggy; "but – but –"

"But you can't," said their mother. "Your duffle coat was just torn: there was nothing missing. These curtains have been *gnawed away*. Big bits are missing, all chewed up at the bottom of those wretched creatures' cage."

"I'll do something, Mum!" cried Sid. "I could buy some more of the red stuff to patch the holes with. I've pocket money saved up. I could buy you new curtains. Mum, I tell you what –"

"No," said his mother, "I'm not thinking of the curtains now."

"But Mum, listen –"

"No," said his mother, "no, no, NO! Not another day in this house if I can help it! They go!"

'But, Mum –"

"THEY GO!"

from *The Battle of Bubble and Squeak* by Philippa Pearce.

Authors such as Jacqueline Wilson and Anne Fine have popularised a relatively new genre in children's literature: realistic stories that raise issues, tackling anything from bereavement to lighter family relationships.

Distinctive qualities of these stories include well-paced dialogue, recognisable settings and strong characterisation – with plenty of opportunities to empathise with the main character. Typically, the story focuses on the character who is grappling with the issue, either by means of a first-person narrative or an all-seeing narrator.

Shared activities

The Suitcase Kid

The issue at the heart of this book – what happens to children in the aftermath of a divorce – is announced starkly in the opening line of this first chapter. Told in the first person, we rapidly learn how resistant Andrea is to her parents' break-up and the comfort that Radish, her toy rabbit, brings her.

Introduce the idea of 'issues' by asking the children what kinds of things Jacqueline Wilson likes to write about. List their ideas as a class reference list of issues. Read the extract through together, then ask the children to re-enact the row between Mum and Dad in pairs, using a copy of the extract.

Still in pairs, ask the children to talk about what they think the issue is and what Andrea's feelings about it are. What do they think Andrea really means when she says that Radish can't bear to hear her parents arguing?

The Battle of Bubble and Squeak

Philippa Pearce's short story explores family relationships through the introduction of pets into the household. Sid brings two gerbils home from school. Knowing his mum won't like them he tries keeping them in the shed, but when it starts to get colder he has to bring them into the house and his secret is discovered. His sisters – Peggy and Amy – love them, but his mum wants them out. This extract depicts a particularly vivid flashpoint, leading to an ultimatum that the gerbils must go.

In contrast to the first extract, this third-person narrative leaves the reader to understand the feelings of the different characters from what they say. After reading the extract, a hot-seating activity can explore this with the children. Ask for a volunteer to adopt the role of Mum or Sid, and invite the children's questions.

Problems and feelings

Talk with the children to try to identify the main issue in *The Suitcase Kid*, then complete the main section of photocopiable page 8 as a shared writing activity to explore each character's feelings provoked by the issue. Try to highlight the distinction between the issue itself, which is common to all the characters, and the feelings generated, which will be unique to each individual. Allocate a character to pairs or larger groups and ask them to explore what the problems and feelings might be for their character. The counsellor should allow a more objective look at the issue.

Who feels what?

Compare the two extracts. Draw attention to the way that *The Battle of Bubble and Squeak* uses action and dialogue to give clues about the characters' feelings, but doesn't reveal everything; the reader is left to infer the rest. How is this different from *The Suitcase Kid*? Photocopiable page 9 asks the children to interpret what the characters are feeling. Ask the children, in pairs, to decide on each character's most revealing piece of speech, justifying their choices as they discuss it.

Taking ideas further

The examples and activities in this section encourage the children to look at some of the principles for writing effectively about issues. It's not an easy area to teach: you are seeking to support the children in both writing a story that is realistic and one that specifically tackles an issue.

As you move the children towards planning their own stories, choosing an issue to write about needs sensitive handling. Develop the class list started earlier to demonstrate the range of options open to the children. The most fruitful writing, though, is likely to come from personal experience, so you might like to suggest that the children use this as their starting point. If this is the case, you will need to be very clear that this is not autobiographical writing, and that the children will need to fictionalise what may be an autobiographical nugget at the heart of their story.

Through the eyes of...

This sheet, which can be worked on independently, aims to draw the children's attention to different narrative devices that can support the development of a story. The top half of photocopiable page 10 explores the notion of a confidante, whether human or not, encouraging the children to think about Andrea's feelings and her relationship with Radish.

Retelling the second extract from Sid's perspective reminds the children of the power of first-person narrative for this kind of writing. Note that Pearce's technique of letting the characters' actions and speech describe their feelings is sophisticated, and one that children may find hard to replicate. A first-person narrative style is probably the easiest approach, at least for a first attempt at this kind of writing.

Writing good stories about issues

The poster on photocopiable page 11 can either be enlarged for the classroom wall or copied so children can have their own reference copy. Each point reminds the children of something that they have looked at when reading the texts and carrying out the activities in this section, and it also anticipates those to come. Encourage the children to use this as a guide throughout the writing process.

Extension ideas

Most importantly, developing this kind of writing should rest on a foundation of reading good quality fiction. The following titles are just a few of the many available.
● *The Eighteenth Emergency* by Betsy Byars (Red Fox) – deals with relationships at school, fear of older children, fear of physical violence
● *The Magic Finger* by Roald Dahl (Puffin Books) – animal rights
● *Goggle Eyes* by Anne Fine (Puffin Books) – mother with new partner
● *The Crowstarver* by Dick King-Smith (Corgi) – mental handicap
● *The Story of Tracy Beaker* by Jacqueline Wilson (Yearling) – child living in a children's home
● *Bed and Breakfast Star* by Jacqueline Wilson (Yearling) – family living in temporary accommodation.

There are suggested drama activities throughout Sections Two and Three, and the more you can include these the better. They are particularly useful for helping the children to empathise with characters and for thinking through ways of developing the plot. Activities such as hot-seating , role-play and freeze-framing (where action is 'frozen' during role-play and the characters are asked to reveal their thoughts) all have important parts to play.

Problems and feelings

The issue in this story is: _____

_____

Andrea

Andrea's main problem is

What does she feel about it?

Mum

The main problem for Mum is

What does she feel about it?

Illustration © 1997, Nick Sharratt

Dad

The main problem for Dad is

What does he feel about it?

Counsellor

The main problem for the counsellor is

What do you think she feels about it?

    writing guides: REALISTIC STORIES

Who feels what?

Mum

What is she feeling? _____

_____

How do we know? _____

_____

_____

What is the most revealing thing that she says?
Write it in the speech bubble.

What is he feeling? _____

_____

How do we know? _____

_____

_____

What is the most revealing thing that he
says? Write it in the speech bubble.

Sid

writing guides: **REALISTIC STORIES**

📖 S C H O L A S T I C **PHOTOCOPIABLE**   9

Through the eyes of...

The Suitcase Kid
Jacqueline Wilson lets us know how important Radish is to Andrea. Work with a partner to decide what Andrea might say to Radish when they get home from the counselling session. What did she think about the counsellor? What worries might she have about the future?

Illustration © 1997, Nick Sharratt

The Battle of Bubble and Squeak
Philippa Pearce's story is written in the third person. Rewrite the incident from Sid's point of view, using the first person. Think about the words you will need to change.

writing guides: REALISTIC STORIES

Writing good stories about issues

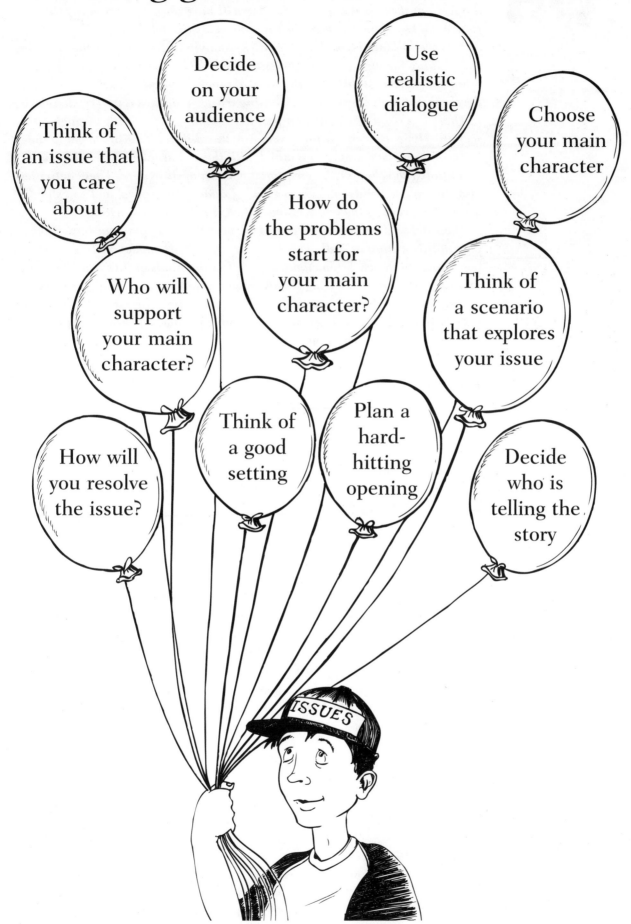

Think of an issue that you care about

Decide on your audience

Use realistic dialogue

Choose your main character

Who will support your main character?

How do the problems start for your main character?

Think of a scenario that explores your issue

How will you resolve the issue?

Think of a good setting

Plan a hard-hitting opening

Decide who is telling the story

ISSUES

SECTION TWO
DEVELOPING WRITING

The texts in Section One should help the children to start thinking of what types of issues they might tackle in their own stories, and ways of looking at the feelings these issues generate. They will have also explored narrative stance – a key element when writing in a realistic style.

This section builds on these ideas with activities that support the children in: thinking through the types of issue they could write about; developing the main character; establishing the roles of other characters; crafting dialogue; developing a realistic setting; and using trigger points as a progression device.

There is a strong emphasis on pair discussion and role-play throughout this section. These are crucial for developing the children's ability to get to the heart of their issue and to empathise with their characters, providing an opportunity to rehearse the emotional content of this genre. These activities also link to the children's own reading of quality literature, and you should always be aware of the connections between reading and writing.

The teacher demonstration strand of shared writing plays an important part in this section as well. This is an opportunity to model writing styles and techniques to the children. You need to plan the kinds of thinking aloud that will enhance such modelling. For example, when demonstrating dialogue writing in 'Get talking!' (pages 14 and 15), you might like to say I've already used 'said', and I want to use another word that suggests how upset the character is – perhaps I could use 'moaned'.

Developing the issue

The first three activities support children's developing understanding of the range of issues they could write about, and in choosing one for their own story. There is the chance for a first go at a piece of writing, which may or may not end up in the final story. Sensitive support may well be needed as children choose their issue.

Choosing an issue could be enhanced further by setting up class debates or persuasive writing activities about common issues (bedtimes, pocket money, or the pros and cons of Andrea moving between parents in *The Suitcase Kid*).

Characterisation

The next two activities help to set up the main and subsidiary characters. The first links the main character with the chosen issue; the second encourages the children to think of possible roles for secondary characters. Some hot-seating work would be useful to develop empathy with the main character.

The dialogue activities that follow also strengthen characterisation. These are embedded in discussion and role-play, and there is reference to the two extracts used in Section One, which make skilled use of dialogue. There is an opportunity for further writing, which may form part of the finished story.

Story setting

'Story setting' provides the children with a way of visualising a realistic setting and, literally, locating their characters. Modelling this kind of activity based on a familiar text may help the children before they embark on their independent efforts.

Trigger points

The 'Trigger points' activity looks particularly at the role of triggers in initiating action. Again, the starting points are examples from children's literature, and there's a chance for the children to attempt an opening paragraph for their story.

writing guides: **REALISTIC STORIES**

THINKING ABOUT ISSUES

WHAT YOU NEED

Photocopiable page 17 cut into scenario cards.

WHAT TO DO

Divide the children into groups of four, and give each group one of the scenario cards from photocopiable page 17. Ask each group to develop a short role-play based around the issue given on their card. Encourage them to think about the characters that will take part in their scenario, the feelings they might have, and how they might demonstrate these (through what they say, how they look and so on). Can they suggest what sides people might take and make these clear in the role-play?

Once the groups have developed their pieces, gather the class together to watch each group's work. Can the children guess what the issues are in each case? As the issues are identified, add them to the class list created earlier (see page 6).

OBJECTIVES

■ To think about a possible range of issues.
■ To understand how issues can be raised in a realistic story.

WHAT'S MY ISSUE?

WHAT YOU NEED

Photocopiable page 18, writing and drawing materials, the class list of issues extended in the previous activity.

WHAT TO DO

Ask the children to work in pairs on a copy each of photocopiable page 18, which allows them to develop a role-play independently, starting from the scenarios on the sheet. Typically, these scenes will focus on a crisis point. Encourage the children to think about characters and how they think and feel in these situations as they fill in the sheet, but not to complete the final box just yet.

When the children have finished their scenarios, spend a few minutes with the whole class looking at all the issues they have explored. Use these to complete the class list of possible issues for the children's own stories, reminding them how they explored these through role-plays and cartoons.

OBJECTIVE

■ To develop consideration of issues.

CHOICES

WHAT YOU NEED

The children's completed copies of photocopiable page 18, the class list of issues from the previous activity, paper, writing materials.

WHAT TO DO

Explain to the children that they are now ready to decide on an issue for their stories. This could be drawn from their work, the class list or their own experience (which may need to be dealt with sensitively). Having chosen their issue, ask them to write it as a title in the middle of a blank piece of paper and brainstorm some of the feelings they associate with the issue.

After the brainstorm, explain to the children that they need to think of a plot for their story that links together some of the ideas from their brainstorm. Using a prompt line such as *It all started when…*, ask the children to use the blank box on photocopiable page 18 to draw a possible scene that might happen in their story. Once they have imagined their scene, ask the children to draft a short paragraph describing it. This will help them to think about the events surrounding the crisis point to be depicted in their story.

OBJECTIVES

■ To choose an issue to write about.
■ To begin thinking about plot.

THE MAIN CHARACTER

WHAT YOU NEED

Photocopiable page 19, writing materials.

WHAT TO DO

Look at an enlarged copy of the photocopiable sheet with the whole class, and ask the children for ideas on how to fill in the boxes. Encourage a range of suggestions, including adjectives (*happy, carefree*), phrases (*doesn't know what to do*), and maybe even catchphrases for the main character. Remind the children about Radish – Andrea's confidante in *The Suitcase Kid* – and suggest that they might like to include a special friend for their main character. Make sure the children understand the role of a confidant(e) – someone or something that is always there for the main character to express his or her feelings – and explain that this could be a toy, a pet or a person. Ask the children to talk about their ideas in pairs before completing their own copy of photocopiable page 19. The bottom of the grid has been left blank for any other categories the children can think of.

OTHER CHARACTERS

WHAT YOU NEED

Photocopiable page 20, writing and drawing materials, scissors, glue.

WHAT TO DO

Talk with the children about some of the other characters they can remember from stories they have read – Andrea's family in *The Suitcase Kid*, for example. Working in pairs, but with a copy of photocopiable page 20 each, ask the children to think of three extra characters for their stories. Using the 'character cards', and through discussion with a partner, encourage them to think of likely roles for these characters before making notes on the sheet.

This work can be extended with the whole class through a hot-seating activity as a plenary. Ask a child to explain one of their extra characters to the rest of the class, then to take the hot seat as their main character. The rest of the class draw on the information to ask questions of the main character (for example, *Why does X always make trouble for you?, How has Y helped you?*). Once the technique has been demonstrated, children could repeat this as independent group work.

GET TALKING! 1

WHAT YOU NEED

Copies of the extracts from pages 4 and 5.

WHAT TO DO

This activity can be organised as a shared reading session. Explain that lively, realistic dialogue is an important feature of writing about issues. Ask the children to look again at the two extracts on pages 4 and 5 and to focus on the speech in each extract, looking at how the authors use dialogue in each case.

From *The Suitcase Kid*, the children should pick up on the use of dialogue in disagreements and as a technique for showing how badly Andrea's mum and dad are getting on. Remind the children of the conversations they wrote between Andrea and Radish on photocopiable page 10. In *The Battle of Bubble and Squeak*, dialogue occurs at a time of crisis and is useful in telling us how the main characters are feeling. Can the children identify special ways that punctuation has been used to enhance the vividness of the dialogue (for example, the use of italic, capital letters, exclamation marks and dashes)?

GET TALKING! 2

WHAT YOU NEED

A set of prompt cards (enough for one per pair) for role-play work, outlining situations involving dialogue (see below), paper, writing and drawing materials, board or flip chart, a prepared section of dialogue based on one of these situations (optional).

OBJECTIVE
■ To develop skills in dialogue writing.

WHAT TO DO

Give each pair of children a prompt card and ask them to use these situations as the basis of a role-play in the form of a conversation between the two characters. Situations on the cards could include: *Mum and Dad have a row over who should go shopping, Two friends work out how to play a trick on their teacher, A customer complains to a shopkeeper about a bar of chocolate that's gone mouldy, Mum tells her child it's time for bed in the middle of a great TV programme.* Choose one or two pairs to share their role-plays with the rest of the class. As the other children listen to the dialogue, ask them to make a list of synonyms for *said* that would match the tone of the conversation (*shouted, moaned, snapped, whispered, retorted* and so on). Make a class list of these for reference later, and ask the children to add to the list as they come across further examples, either from their own reading or from a thesaurus.

Choose a section of dialogue from one of the role-plays (or use your own prepared section) and model writing a few lines of the dialogue on the board. Point out features such as the use of punctuation for emphasis; use of synonyms for *said*; simple, snappy sentences to inject pace; repetition; and how to convey emotion. You may also want to revise punctuation conventions for direct speech, but bear in mind that the main focus here should be on the content, pace and focus of the dialogue.

For the plenary session, ask the children to prepare a poster with the title 'Tips for writing good dialogue'. Display the poster, and encourage the children to add to it as they come across other features of dialogue in their day-to-day reading.

GET TALKING! 3

WHAT YOU NEED

Photocopiable page 21, writing materials.

OBJECTIVE
■ To bring together characters and dialogue.

WHAT TO DO

This sheet builds directly on the previous two activities, encouraging the children to begin practising their dialogue-writing skills by setting up possible scenarios for their characters. This will also help them to empathise with their characters, consider the feelings that accompany speech and reinforce vocabulary work on synonyms for *said*.

Encourage the children to work independently on this sheet, choosing two of the characters from their story, building dialogue in the spaces provided but also noting the feelings behind what they say and using *said* synonyms by filling in the box underneath the speech. Before they start the activity, you could suggest some possible opening lines to help the children start their dialogue, for example: *'You are so wrong...', 'Right, either you...', 'I'm going to tell you something I shouldn't...', 'You'll never guess who I've just seen...'* and *'Great T-shirt!'*.

writing guides: **REALISTIC STORIES**

STORY SETTING

WHAT YOU NEED

A3 paper, writing and drawing materials, a prepared story map (see below).

WHAT TO DO

A story map is a simple sketch of the areas described in a story and highlights key aspects of the settings. A story map for *The Suitcase Kid*, for example, would feature the parents' new homes and Mulberry Cottage. *The Battle of Bubble and Squeak* also lends itself very well to this, as does the opening chapter of Betsy Byars' *The Eighteenth Emergency*.

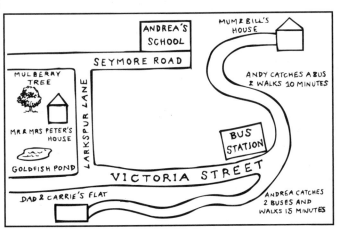

Explain the idea of story maps to the children. If they have not worked with these before you might like to model building one for *The Suitcase Kid* in a shared session, encouraging the children to contribute settings to the map, based on the sketch on the left.

Give each child a blank sheet of paper, and tell them that they should create a story map for their own story, starting with the main character's home. Encourage them to think about where their other characters might live, as well as adding places of significance (the school, park, shops or swimming pool, for example) to their map. The map should be annotated as fully as possible, including reference to some of the possible scenes they looked at in 'Choices' on page 13 (for example, *main character has row with friend in park*).

TRIGGER POINTS

WHAT YOU NEED

OBJECTIVE

■ To look at ways of initiating a story's problem or conflict.

Copies of photocopiable page 22, writing materials; a selection of story books (not necessarily about issues) that contain a range of opening techniques, including those that move straight into the action (such as *The Iron Man* by Ted Hughes, or *Bill's New Frock* by Anne Fine) and others where setting and character are established first (such as *The Suitcase Kid*); a copy of *The Battle of Bubble and Squeak*.

WHAT TO DO

Talk with the children about story openings. Ask pairs to read the opening paragraphs of two or three novels from your selection, and to discuss the different techniques authors use to get their stories started.

Together, read the opening paragraph of *The Suitcase Kid* from photocopiable page 4. Point out how Jacqueline Wilson announces the issue in the very first sentence, then proceeds to fill in details about the characters.

Go on to read the opening lines from a copy of *The Battle of Bubble and Squeak*. Ask the children what device has been used here and introduce the term 'trigger point', explaining if necessary that it is a technique that unsettles the way things are and prompts the action of a story. Explain that trigger points can occur at the very start of a story or some way into the opening, and that they are just one way of instigating the action.

Ask the children to work on photocopiable page 22. Identifying the trigger points could be done in pairs, but the final section is for individual work. Explain that this will not necessarily be the opening they eventually use for their story, but is a chance to try out ideas.

Thinking about issues

Family conflict
I really want a new games console but I'm not allowed one.

Bullying
I knew that Darren was having a really bad time with the kids from Greenfield School.

Friendship
My friend Tracy won't even talk to me these days.

Family rows
When my dad's car got nicked there was a BIG row!

Loss
When my dog died I was really sad.

Animal rights
I just don't think it's right to eat meat.

What's my issue?

What might happen in each of these issues?
Try to draw and caption a scene that illustrates each of these
situations. The first one has been done for you.

| **Family jealousy** | **Bullying** | **Family row** |

Think of your own idea for a scene to draw in the last box.

| **Loss** | **Friendship** | |

The main character

The main character in my story is _____

He or she is _____ years old.

The problem the character faces is _____

_____

Draw your character in the space, and use this table to help you to think about what your character was like before the problem started and how things change as the story progresses.

	Before	During	After
Feelings			
Relationship with parents			
Relationship with friends			
Relationship with siblings			

My character's special confidant(e) is _____

_____

Other characters

Think of three more important characters for your story.
Choose each character's role from the list at the bottom. Draw their pictures and jot down some ideas about them. Think about:

- How does he or she support the main character?
- How does he or she make things difficult for the main character?
- How are they involved in the problem?

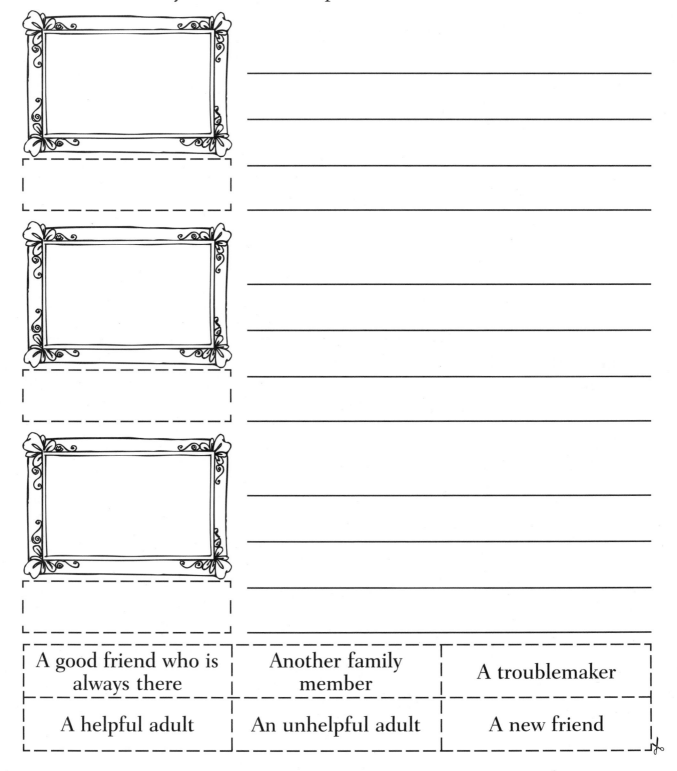

| A good friend who is always there | Another family member | A troublemaker |
| A helpful adult | An unhelpful adult | A new friend |

writing guides: **REALISTIC STORIES**

Get talking!

Choose one of your extra characters and have a go at writing some dialogue between him or her and your main character. Think about what each person will be feeling as he or she speaks.

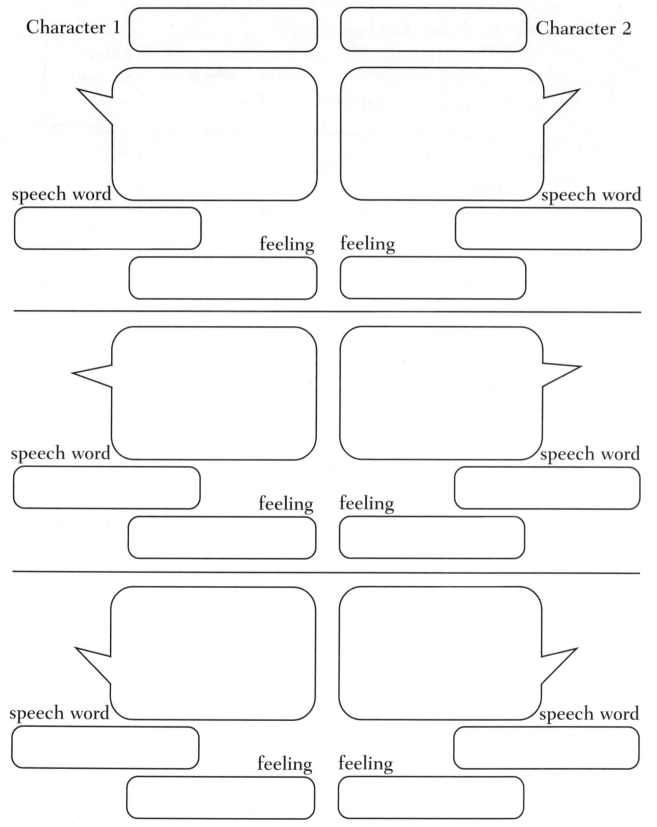

Character 1

Character 2

speech word

speech word

feeling

feeling

speech word

speech word

feeling

feeling

speech word

speech word

feeling

feeling

Trigger points

Trigger points are a very good way of getting your story going. Read these two opening paragraphs and highlight the trigger point in each.

> *I was playing on my computer. I'd done my homework, won some new cards and had baked beans for tea. Everything was great until Mum came upstairs and said, "Gary's here!" I gulped. Gary was the last person in the world I wanted to see right now. He'd never forgiven me for what happened last summer.*

> *Our new house was brilliant. For the first time in my life I had my own room and didn't have to share with my little brother Arnie. We were close to my best friend and I could walk to the shops on my own. Then one night Dad came home looking terrible. Mum asked me to run to the shop for chips but I knew she just wanted me out of the way.*

Here are some more trigger points. Choose one of these, or write your own, and put it into an opening paragraph for your story.

Everything was going fine until…
I knew straight away that something was wrong…
Suddenly everything changed…
One minute we were all happy, the next…

writing guides: **REALISTIC STORIES**

The children have looked at models of realistic writing in Section One, and have carried out a range of planning activities in Section Two. This section allows them to orchestrate these elements into individual stories organised in mini-chapters. To help them, the children should keep all their earlier work in one, accessible folder so they can refer to it, and the extracts from pages 4 and 5 should be on display in the classroom, along with the poster on page 11. Although the emphasis in this section is on individual, independent writing, the role of discussion with a partner makes a significant contribution to work at this stage.

By now the children should have chosen an issue for their story and have clear notes on characters, setting, dialogue and trigger points. They may have also had a first go at writing small sections of their stories, and can choose whether or not to incorporate these into their final versions.

The intention is that all the children should write 'mini-chapter' stories. The length and complexity of these chapters will vary according to individual needs, but the four-step element described in this section, which offers a structure for developing the plot, should be maintained for all.

Story steps and Where have I got to?

These two activities allow the children to take stock of their ideas and develop the overall shape of their story. The poster on photocopiable pages 24 and 25 is ideal for enlarging as a model in a whole-class shared writing session. At this stage, it is important that the children are given the opportunity to talk their story through with a partner to gain feedback and suggestions for improvements. Consider also, with permission, displaying successfully completed planners for the rest of the class to see. (Some children may be willing to share incomplete planners to elicit ideas from their classmates.) Remember that, while the structure offered should be helpful, it is the surrounding discussion that will enable children to really flesh their stories out. Photocopiable page 26 provides a checklist that should reassure the children about how much they have already done, and will help to extend their thinking about audience, narrative stance, title and ending for their story.

Getting going

Photocopiable page 27 can be used to kick-start the actual story-writing process. It offers children three different ways of introducing their issue and main character, which they can choose from when starting their story. As the children complete this activity, encourage them to refer to the notes they made in Section Two about issues, settings and characters. With these instructions in hand, and with a reminder of their work in Section Two, the children can write the first chapter of their story.

Planning a chapter in detail and Key dialogue

These two generic photocopiables offer extra support to children, and can be used as needed. Photocopiable page 28 is a support structure for each chapter of the children's stories, and the worksheet on photocopiable page 29 provides help in writing passages of dialogue for the story, but also encouraging empathy with the characters and thought about the feelings behind the dialogue. When completing 'Key dialogue', point out to the children that they should try and describe the feelings of their character in the thought bubble, as well as what they say in the speech bubble. Each of these worksheets could be used with less confident children or if anybody gets stuck on a particular section of their story.

Story steps

Use these planning steps to make notes about how your story will unfold.
Make notes next to each rung to see your story build up.

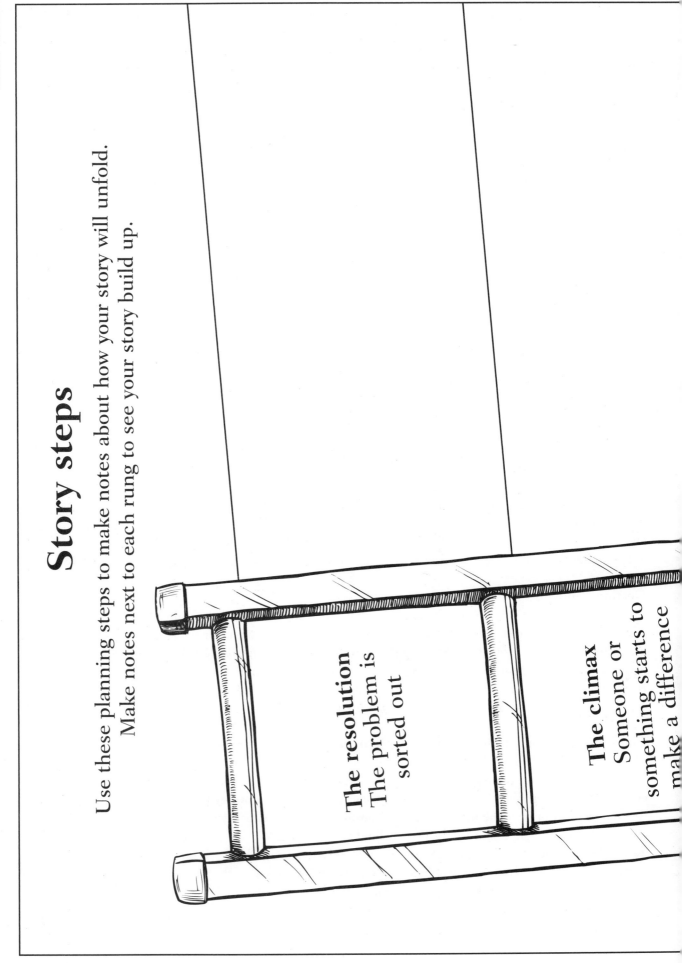

The resolution
The problem is
sorted out

The climax
Someone or
something starts to
make a difference

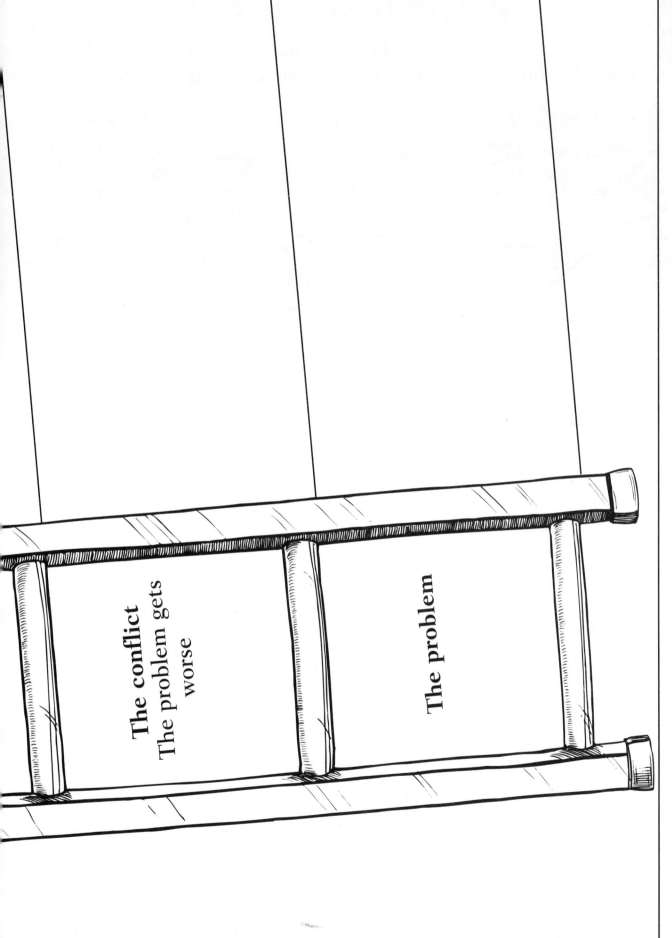

The conflict
The problem gets worse

The problem

Where have I got to?

Use this checklist to remind yourself of what you've already done towards writing your story, and what you still need to think about.

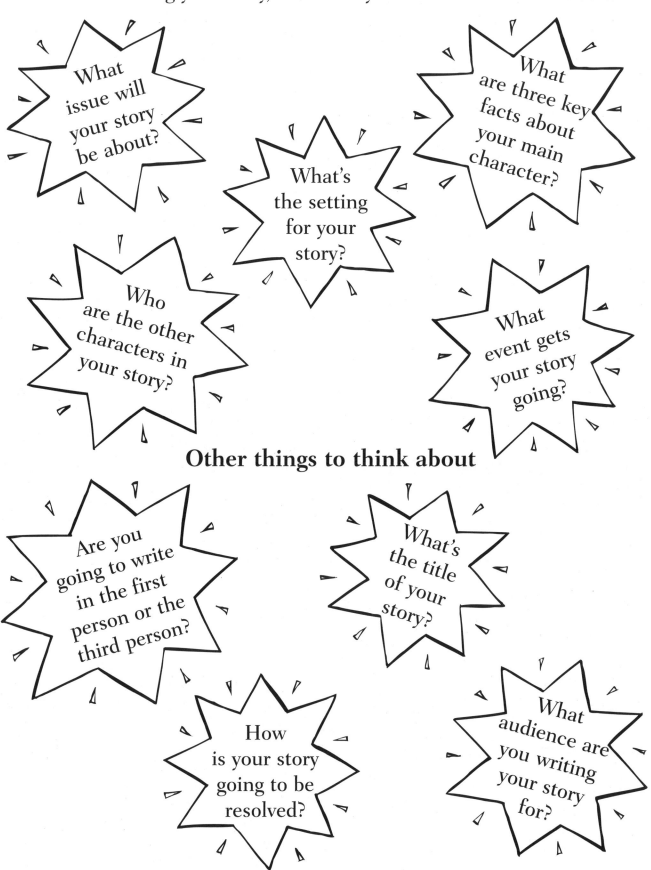

What issue will your story be about?

What's the setting for your story?

What are three key facts about your main character?

Who are the other characters in your story?

What event gets your story going?

Other things to think about

Are you going to write in the first person or the third person?

What's the title of your story?

How is your story going to be resolved?

What audience are you writing your story for?

writing guides: REALISTIC STORIES

Getting going

How are you going to introduce your issue to the reader? Try writing an opening paragraph in each of these ways.

You could…

…use a flashback to explain something that happened in the past to your main character. Try a flashback here. ▶	

…tell the reader what the main character is thinking. Try writing the character's thoughts here. ▶	

…use a piece of dialogue with another character to reveal the problem. Try writing some dialogue here. ▶	

Choose your favourite opening paragraph, and use your ideas about characters and settings to help you write the first chapter of your story.

Planning a chapter in detail

Use these questions to help you plan what's going to happen
in the next chapter of your story.

What's this chapter going to be called?	The main point of the chapter is
Which characters appear in this chapter?	How does the central character feel at the beginning of the chapter?
How does he or she feel by the end of the chapter?	Make a note on your story map where the action takes place in this chapter.
What is the main development in this chapter?	What happens at the end of the chapter? Your reader should want to find out what happens next!

Key dialogue

This sheet will help you plan key bits of dialogue for your story. You can use it for any conversations that take place at important points in your story. Write your dialogue in the speech bubbles, and think about what your characters are thinking at the same time.

Point in the story that you've got to: _____

_____

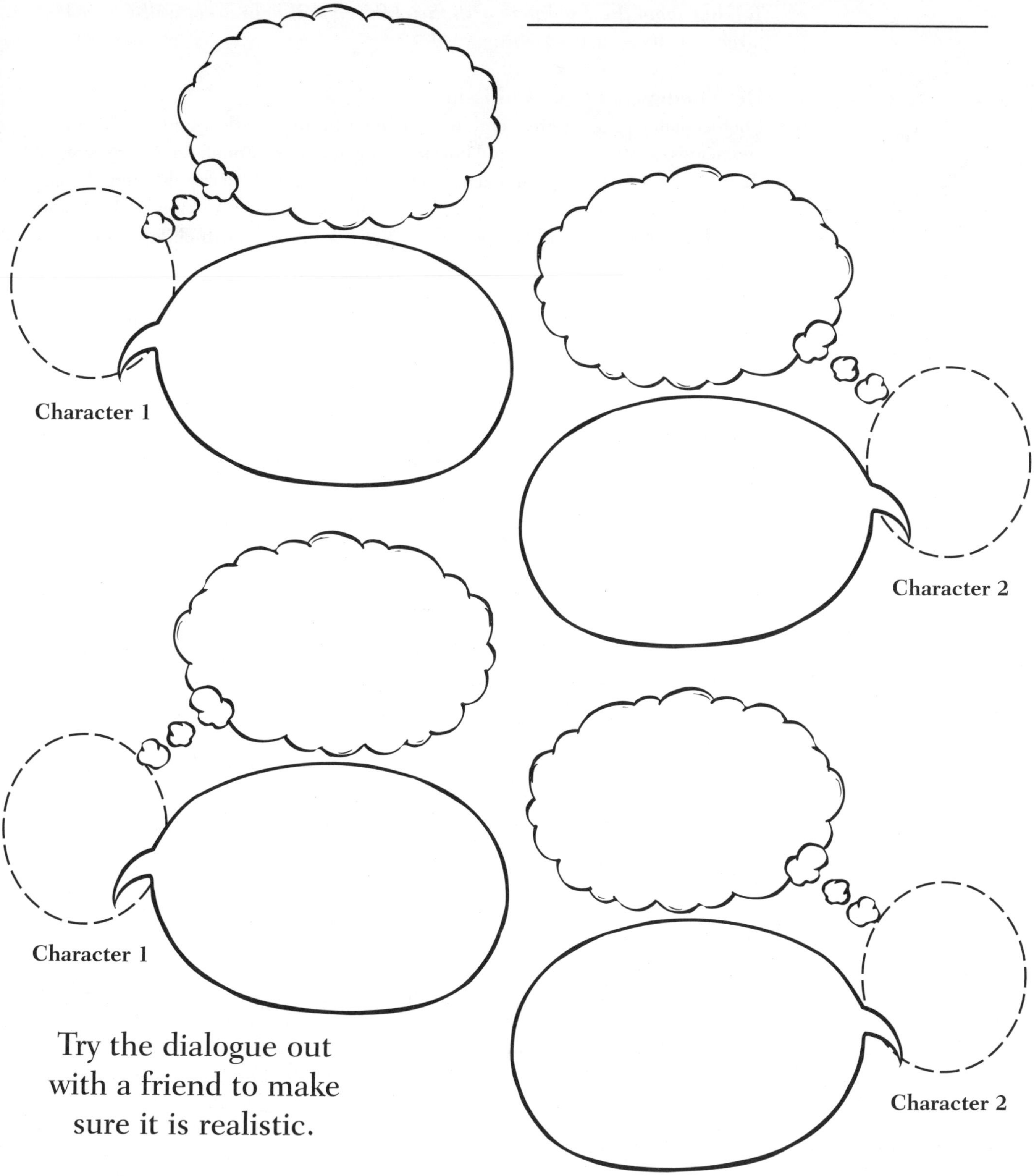

Character 1

Character 2

Character 1

Try the dialogue out with a friend to make sure it is realistic.

Character 2

Having planned and written their story over the past three sections, the following activities will help the children to reflect on different elements of their writing: character, opening, plot, setting and dialogue.

As well as the children's own thoughts, you might like to use the following pointers in assessment, drawing evidence from both Sections Two and Three, when looking at the completed stories:
- *credible, empathetic characters*
- *well established, realistic settings*
- *appropriate use of trigger points and/or flashbacks*
- *believable and lively dialogue*
- *a well-developed and sustained plot.*

Talking about these pointers with the children will help to set well-focused targets for their future writing.

Developing character and issue

Photocopiable page 31 gives children the opportunity to reflect on how their main character's emotions change, and how the issue develops through their story. Suggest that they start by highlighting key passages in their stories, using different colours for points about character and issue, then fill in the sheet, identifying the key points in each chapter. This can be done individually or in pairs, with children swapping stories, offering feedback and helping each other find the key passages to add to the chart.

You may want to add additional adjectives to the wordbank that are more appropriate to an individual story.

Help cards

The cards on photocopiable page 32 provide a framework for paired review of the children's stories, and are ideal for providing feedback and setting targets for improvement at the end of an independent writing session. Alternatively, use the cards in one-off 'improving writing' slots, with pairs of children using the questions on the cards as prompts for discussion of each other's work.

Other activities

There are many other ways in which children can reflect on their stories and think of ways to improve their work.
- Ask the children to write a blurb for the back of their story, or to devise publicity material (a flyer maybe) that can be sent to another class in advance of a special reading of some of the stories. It is important that children get to try their stories out on their intended audience to get some feedback to develop their writing.
- Using the completed stories, ask the class to look again at some of the issues raised. Debating the rights and wrongs of a particular dilemma from the children's stories will strengthen the individual author's esteem and help strengthen the sense of an authentic audience.
- Ask the children to devise a 'style guide' for another class on writing a realistic story, detailing what they have learned while writing their own stories.
- Hold a class awards ceremony and award prizes – 'Best issue book of the year', 'Prize for excellent characterisation', 'Dramatic dialogue winner', 'Plausible plots' – to each other's stories. Ask the children to write judges' reports on some of the stories before making the awards.

Developing character and issue

In the first column, choose adjectives from the wordbank that describe how your main character feels in each chapter of your story. Is there anything you can add that will improve your writing about how the character is feeling?

In the second column, make notes about how the issue is developed in each chapter. Could you add anything to make the issue clearer for the reader?

	Character	Issue
Chapter 1		
Chapter 2		
Chapter 3		
Chapter 4		

Wordbank

distressed

uneasy

relieved

content

relaxed

nervous

edgy

angry

exasperated

uncertain

miserable

confused

Help cards

Use these help cards with a writing partner.
Ask each other the questions to give feedback and ideas
on how to improve parts of your stories.

The opening
● Read the opening paragraph aloud.

● Is there a part you especially like?

● Is there anything that could be improved?

The plot
● What is the outline of your plot?

● Is it a realistic plot?

● What is your favourite chapter ending?

● Are there any bits that need working on?

The setting
● Which part of the story describes the setting?

● What is your favourite thing about the setting?

● Is there anything about the setting that isn't believable?

Dialogue
● What is your favourite section of dialogue?

● Read the chosen section together. What is good about it?

● Could it be improved at all? Is there a particular section that needs more work?

writing guides: **REALISTIC STORIES**